THE one hundred greatest MOMENTS IN Football

THE one hundred greatest
MOMENTS IN
Football

This bo...
th...

TIM VIGON

WITH A FOREWORD BY
RODNEY MARSH

generation
PUBLICATIONS

Written by Nick Brownlee

Designed by Robert Kelland and Adrian Waddington

With thanks to
Phil McNeill, Eve Cossins, Mark Crossland, Deanne Pearson and Catherine McNeill;
and to Julie Foster and Rob Brown at Colour Systems

Special thanks to Rodney Marsh

Published by David Crowe and Mark Peacock

First published in Great Britain in 1999 by Generation Publications
11-12 Tottenham Mews, London W1P 9PJ

generationgroup@btconnect.com

Text copyright © Generation Publications

A catalogue record for this title is available from the British Library

ISBN 1 903009 17 0

Production by Mike Powell & Associates (01494 676891)
Origination by Colour Systems Ltd, London
Printed and bound in Spain by Bookprint, S.L.,Barcelona

All photographs except those listed below are from Allsport, with thanks to Rob Harborne;
Empics images appear on pages 54, 76 and 81, with thanks to Ian Lilley;
ColorSport images appear on pages 18, 63, 87, 92, 93, 98, 102 and 108

Page 1: Diego Maradona and the Argentinian team during Italia '90
Page 2: The White Horse Final – PC George Scorey and Billy clear the
Wembley pitch before Bolton take on West Ham in the 1923 FA Cup Final
Page 3: Paul Gascoigne's World Cup ends in tears

Contents

• Foreword •

by Rodney Marsh

Sport has produced many great moments. We all have our personal favourites and we all remember them in different ways. For me, Gordon Banks' save in the 1970 World Cup Finals stands out: perhaps because Brazil were my favourite team and because Pele was the greatest player in the world.

The reason I remember it so vividly is because there were countless times that Gordon Banks had made brilliant saves from me. It was a pleasure to play alongside him for England and to witness at first hand how he made the most difficult saves look easy.

But 'The Banks Save' isn't alone. There were many great moments before that, and many since - like David Beckham's goal from behind the halfway line against Wimbledon on the opening day of the season three years ago. Whatever your personal favourite, enjoy the following one hundred.

Save of the century: Banks denying Pele in the 1970 World Cup is Marsh's favourite moment

Van Basten blaster
Holland 2 USSR 0 1988

The Euro Championships in Germany had all started so ignominiously for Holland and their striker Marco Van Basten. After losing to the much-fancied, powerful Soviets in the first game, Van Basten – who had missed the match – was so teed off he wanted to go home. He only changed his mind when that great Dutch legend of the 1970s, Johann Cruyff, put his arm around the tall striker and told him that this was the perfect stage to confirm that he was the greatest goalscorer in the world.

1

Van Basten did not disappoint. With the likes of Gullit, Rijkaard and Muhren alongside, the Orange Army swept all before them in the qualifying rounds to reach the final

Van Basten *factfile*

Born: 31.10.64, Utrecht, Holland
Position: Centre Forward
Games: 280   **Goals:** 218
Clubs: Ajax, Milan
International
Appearances/Goals: 58/24
Career highlights: European Footballer of the Year 1988, 1989 and 1993

'Marco is a symbol for all the attackers, even myself, everybody wants to be like Marco Van Basten.
He's the greatest.'
George Weah
on Van Basten after
replacing him at AC Milan

against their old enemy the USSR. Holland won convincingly – and it was Van Basten who provided the gobsmacking moment.

From a deep cross from Arnold Muhren, Van Basten, unmarked on the right of the penalty area, connected perfectly with the ball. From the tightest of angles, the ball flew back across the goal and into the opposite top corner. There was stunned silence before the crowd exploded at the sensational goal.

Marco Van Basten lifts the European Championship trophy, after contributing to the win with his spectacular volley from an amazingly acute angle

A late KO

Liverpool 0 Arsenal 2 1989

The equation was quite simple. To wrest the First Division title from Liverpool's grasp, Arsenal had to win their last game of the season by two clear goals. What complicated matters somewhat was that their opponents were Liverpool themselves – and the venue was Anfield.

Nonetheless, in surely the most nailbiting title showdown of all time, Arsenal poured forward in the last minute of the match – nay, the season – leading one goal to nil but still requiring a second. Suddenly, the ball was in the box at the feet of Michael Thomas. Surely he couldn't... As the red shirts flung themselves desperately in the way, Thomas coolly despatched the ball into the net past Grobbelaar. The title was Arsenal's in the most dramatic way possible.

Thomas and Martin Hayes enjoy their title win

Thomas scores Arsenal's vital second goal to snatch the Championship away from Liverpool

Gazza's night to remember

England 4 Holland 1 1996

Euro 96 generated the kind of national football frenzy that hadn't been experienced in these shores since the World Cup of thirty years before. And, as with '66, much of it was down to the progress of the England team.

Having failed to qualify for the World Cup in the USA, England, now managed by Terry Venables, surprised even themselves with a brand of enterprising football few believed them capable of.

3

With each passing game, the excitement mounted. But it was against Holland in the group match, that it all came together for 90 sensational minutes. Not only were the Dutch outscored 4-1, they were utterly outplayed. England's glorious dominance was summed when the electric Gazza darted into the penalty area and squared the ball to Sheringham.

Instead of shooting, Sheringham deftly sidefooted the ball to the lurking Shearer, who unleashed a right-footed pile-driver inside the near post.

> *"Maybe he knows something.*
>
> *He's supposed to be able to look into the future, isn't he?"*
>
> Terry Venables on claims in Glenn Hoddle's World Cup Diary that Venables wanted his old England coaching job back

Darren Anderton, Paul Gascoigne, Teddy Sheringham and Steve McManaman celebrate

Victory is sealed and Paul Gascoigne lets everyone know about England's fourth goal

England v Holland *factfile*

England's record v Holland

Played	Won	Drawn	Lost	Goals For	Goals Against
13	5	5	3	22	15

Biggest victory: 8-2, Huddersfield, 27.11.46
Biggest defeat: 3-1, Dusseldorf, Germany, 15.6.88

Southgate's night to forget

England 1 Germany 1 1996

"Football is a simple game where 22 players play against each other and in the end Germany wins."
Gary Lineker
1996

Gareth Southgate is consoled after his penalty miss. The stigma of the missed penalty can blight a player's life – ask Roberto Baggio and Chris Waddle – but at least Southgate had the guts to take a penalty, while certain more experienced players watched

England, Germany, and penalty shoot-outs. A potent mixture which always seems to leave England with an almighty hangover. They did for England in Italia 90 and they did for them here in the semi-final of Euro 96. Having clung on through the nerve-wracking tension of golden goals – which indeed England should have won – and survived the first batch of penalties, it was down to the old familiar sudden-death scenario which has become such a part of the English psyche.

This time the fall-guy was the unfortunate Gareth Southgate. The rangy central defender seemed to be trying to place his penalty, but instead he stubbed a weak daisy-cutter, upon which German keeper Illgner gratefully pounced. England were out – but at least Southgate would go on to make a few bob recalling his penalty blunder in a series of Pizza Hut adverts.

England v Germany *factfile*

England's record v Germany
(not including when Germany was split)

Played	Won	Drawn	Lost	Goals For	Goals Against
6	2	2	2	14	10

Biggest victory: 6-3, Berlin, 14.5.38
Biggest defeat: 2-1, Detroit, 19.6.93

Houghton gets Irish eyes smiling

Republic of Ireland 1 Italy 0 1994

There were 90,000 spectators in new York's Giants Stadium – and 40,000 were Irish. They were there for the *craic*, the Guinness and for a damn fine time. Few watching this World Cup group match expected the Republic to seriously trouble Italy, with the likes of Maldini, Baresi and Baggio.

Jack Charlton's team knew only one way to play, however, and their in-yer-face harrying soon had the strutting Azurri peacocks reeling. And their feathers were well and truly ruffled after just 12 minutes when diminutive midfielder Ray Houghton picked up the ball 25 yards out and, after a brief sideways shuffle, looked up and saw Italian goalkeeper Pagliuca off his line. Houghton's lob seemed to hang in the air for ever before dipping sweetly into the unguarded net.

Below: Gianluca Pagliuca cannot stop Houghton's dipping lob from going in. Right: Pat Bonner and Gary Kelly celebrate after the final whistle

"If in winning the game we only finish with a draw, we would be fine."
Jack Charlton, Republic of Ireland manager

Magic Magyars
England 3 Hungary 6 1953

The match at Wembley was billed as a friendly – and Hungary certainly had a smile on their face as they gave England a complete thrashing by 6-3. Mind you, such was the quality of their display that grey November day that even die-hard Three Lions supporters were throwing their caps in the air.

Led by the barrel-chested Ferenc Puskas, the 'Magic Magyars' gave a display of previously unseen imagination, audacity and ferocious intent that completely outshone England's mighty trio of Wright, Matthews and Finney. Their third goal, a stunning drag-back and shot by Puskas himself, summed up the occasion.

It was England's first home defeat – and to prove it was no fluke, Hungary hammered them 7-1 in Budapest the following year.

England v Hungary *factfile*

England's record v Hungary

Played	Won	Drawn	Lost	Goals For	Goals Against
20	13	2	5	50	27

Biggest victory: 7-0, Budapest, 10.6.08
Biggest defeat: 7-1, Budapest, 23.5.54

Right: The calm before the storm. The Hungary team line up meekly for the pre-match presentation at Wembley, but there was certainly nothing meek about them when they got out on the pitch

They always score!

Bayern Munich 1 Manchester United 2 1999

Sheringham races off after scoring Manchester United's equaliser with only minutes remaining

Solskjaer sweeps the ball in from close range to win the European Cup for Manchester United and devastate the Bayern Munich players and fans

*"The Cup will only be six feet away
from you at the end of the night.
If you lose, you can't even touch it."*
Alex Ferguson at half-time in the European Cup Final

They must score. They always score!' Thus commentator Clive Tyldesley's prophetic words heralded one of the most extraordinary smash-and-grab acts in football.

Trailing 1-0 in the European Cup Final, United were only seconds from defeat. But the Germans, having run the game since scoring in the first half, were being fatally arrogant, even waving to the crowd as the clock ticked by. Teddy Sheringham was less than impressed by this behaviour and was psyched to the hilt when he and Ole Gunnar Solskjaer came on as Alex Ferguson's last throw of the dice.

Their impact was immediate and dramatic. From a corner, the ball bobbled to the edge of the area. Ryan Giggs fired in a shot and, from less than three yards, Sheringham helped it into the back of the net.

United were not finished. From another corner, Sheringham's back-header fell to Solskjaer, who from the same distance stuck out a foot and diverted the ball into the roof of the net.

There was never a prettier sight to English football fans than that of the distraught Germans barely able to scrape themselves up off the turf before the final whistle confirmed United's historic treble.

That Save

Brazil 1 England 0 1970

Gordon Banks launches himself to pull off a miraculous save from Pele's header

Even now, watching it on blurry video-tape, it is a goal all the way. Jairzinho's cross, Pele's athletic leap, and a bullet header arrowing at 100mph for the bottom right corner. Time seems to stand still.

Yet suddenly amid the frozen figures in white and canary yellow, there is a flash of blue as Gordon Banks launches himself almost the width of the goalmouth to somehow get his hand to the ball and palm it up and over the bar.

In the second half, this classic World Cup group match between the holders – England – and the eventual champions was sealed by Jairzinho's goal, created by Tostao. England piled on the pressure but Brazil held out.

England v Brazil *factfile*

England's record v Brazil

Played	Won	Drawn	Lost	Goals For	Goals Against
19	3	7	9	16	26

Biggest victory: 4-2, Wembley, 9.5.56
Biggest defeat: 5-1, Rio de Janeiro, 30.5.64

Gazza magic

England 2 Scotland 0 1996

*I*t is a bad two minutes to be a Scotland supporter packed into Wembley Stadium for the Euro 96 group match against the Auld Enemy. First, the normally-reliable midfielder Gary McAllister watches aghast as David Seaman punches away his

> *"This is an unusual Scotland side because they have good players."*
> Javier Clemente, Spanish Coach, on Scotland's 1996 under-21 side

penalty kick. Next, England clear the resulting corner upfield quickly to where the much-derided Paul Gascoigne suddenly has jet engines in his boots.

As Colin Hendry backs off, Gascoigne takes the ball in his stride and lobs it casually over the retreating defender's head. As Hendry flounders, looking for the ball, Gazza has already pounced in good time to hammer the ball past the stunned Andy Goram in the Scotland

Paul Gascoigne takes a drink to celebrate his brilliant goal. Gazza's method of celebration was a pointed message to the tabloid newspapers who had recently printed pictures of him enjoying the same treatment – but with different drinks – in the 'Dentist's Chair' in a bar in Hong Kong

net. Euphoria erupts among the Sassenachs.

The delirious Gazza, meanwhile, is flat on his back with his England colleagues squirting water into his open mouth. Sensational goal, sensational celebration.

England v Scotland *factfile*

England's record v Scotland

Played	Won	Drawn	Lost	Goals For	Goals Against
108	44	24	40	190	168

Biggest victory: 9-3, Wembley, 15.4.61
Biggest defeat: 7-2, Hampden Park, 2.3.1878

Armstrong's smash and grab

Spain 0 Northern Ireland 1 1982

10

FUJI FILM METAXA Canon Copiers

Gerry Armstrong blasts the ball in from close range. This proved to be the decisive goal that knocked out the hosts, Spain, in the 1982 World Cup finals

Billy Bingham's men were so delighted to have made the finals of the 1982 World Cup in Spain, they would quite happily have made up the numbers and flown home after the first round. Instead, the Irish ended up top of their group – and were the architects of one of the biggest shocks in World Cup history when they over-turned the hosts in the cauldron of Valencia. When Spanish goalkeeper Arconada could only palm away a hopeful Irish cross, Gerry Armstrong was on hand to hammer home the winner. The goal was by no means an aesthetic classic ... but who cares?

Trautmann breaks neck and plays on

Manchester City 3 Birmingham City 1 1956

Above: 1953 Trautmann saves for Man City v West Ham. Right; Trautmann receiving medical attention to his neck in the 1956 FA Cup Final

FA Cup *factfile*

Manchester City have appeared in 8 finals and won the cup on 4 occasions, the last victory being in 1969, 1-0 v Leicester. The last appearance was in 1981 when they lost 3-2 to Spurs in the replay after a 1-1 draw. **Birmingham City** have appeared in two finals losing both, 3-1 to Manchester City (1956) and 2-1 to West Bromwich Albion in 1931.

Manchester City's tall German goalkeeper Bert Trautmann got through the whole of the 1956 FA Cup Final despite suffering great pain after two brave saves at the feet of Birmingham City players. In fact, it was a full three days later that he was forced to go to hospital where X-rays showed he had a broken neck. Trautmann always maintained that he would do it all again if it meant he received a coveted winner's medal.

The final score in the match was Manchester City 3 (Hayes, Dyson, Johnstone), Birmingham City 1 (Kinsey).

The White Horse Final

Bolton Wanderers 2 West Ham 0 1923

12

Of all the heroes to grace Wembley's turf, by far the most extraordinary appeared once, didn't get among the goals, but, for the best part of 40 minutes, commanded the pitch to such an extent that, without him, Bolton Wanderers might never have won the FA Cup. The hero's name was Billy, and he was a huge white police horse ridden by PC George Scorey. And it was largely thanks to this pair that the 1923 Cup Final went ahead at all.

The game was the very first Wembley final itself. Such was the excitement before the event – not just because of the match but also because of the newly-completed stadium, advertised as "the greatest of its kind" – that the numbers who converged on it that warm spring afternoon exceeded even the wildest expectations.

Officially, the crowd was 127,000, the stadium's capacity at the time. Unofficially, it was at least twice that, with some estimates putting it as high as 300,000. With thousands spilling on to the pitch, it seemed inconceivable that the match would go ahead.

Until, that is, PC Scorey and his horse – plus a few mounted colleagues – cut a swathe

The start was delayed 90 minutes as the huge crowds were crammed into the stands and squeezed around the edge of the pitch

through the crowd and began to restore order. At 3.46pm, with hundreds of fans squeezed right up to the touchline, the game miraculously kicked off.

Ninety minutes later (the teams didn't dare leave the pitch for a half-time break), Bolton had beaten West Ham 2-0.

FA Cup *factfile*

Bolton Wanderers have won the Cup on four occasions and appeared in seven finals. Their last victory came in their last appearance, 2-0 v Manchester United (1958).

West Ham have appeared in four finals and won on three occasions, the last appearance and victory coming in 1980 with a 1-0 win over Arsenal – the last Second Division club to win.

Out of play

Newcastle United 1 Arsenal 0 1932

Newcastle United wrestled the FA Cup from hot favourites Arsenal with a goal which was to have fans talking for years. The ball, as a Pathe newsreel proved afterwards, had gone way out of play before United's Jack Allen whacked it into the Arsenal net. Only the referee saw otherwise. "As God is my judge, the ball was in play," he insisted afterwards.

FA Cup *factfile*

Newcastle United and Arsenal are two of the most successful teams in the history of the FA Cup.

Newcastle United have appeared in 12 finals and won on six occasions, their last victory coming in 1955, 3-1 v Manchester City.

Arsenal have appeared in 13 finals winning on seven occasions, the last one being a 2-0 victory over Newcastle United in 1998.

Newcastle United players are congratulated by fans on their way down the steps after beating Arsenal 2-1, thanks to the referee's bad decision for their first goal

13

Lineker's hat-trick

England 3 Poland 0 1986

England v Poland *factfile*					
England's record v Poland					
Played	Won	Drawn	Lost	Goals For	Goals Against
14	8	5	1	23	8

Biggest victory: 3-0, Monterrey, 11.6.86,
Wembley, 3.6.59, and Wembley, 8.9.93
Biggest defeat: 2-0, Chorzow, 6.6.73

After the first two group games of Mexico '86, it seemed inconceivable that England would progress to the second round, let alone reach the heights of the quarter-finals. A defeat against Portugal was followed by a dismal goalless draw against Morocco. But the sending-off of Ray Wilkins in that last game was, ironically, to provide the spur which saw England transformed into world-beaters against the Poles.

In his place, Bobby Robson selected the underrated Peter Beardsley.

With Beardsley's astute prompting, Gary Lineker profited with a hat-trick within 34 minutes. The pick of his goals was the first

after just eight minutes. Beardsley's pass set Steve Hodge free on the left, the long cross was directed with pinpoint accuracy, and Lineker slid in from six yards to hammer the ball into the roof of the net.

"Gary always weighed up his options, especially when he had no choice."

Kevin Keegan

Far left: Gary Lineker scores the first goal.
Top: Lineker (10) waits to pounce for the third goal of his hat-trick

The burst ball

Derby County 1 Charlton Athletic 0 (aet) 1946

*I*n the first post-war FA Cup Final, Derby County needed extra time before seeing off Charlton Athletic. Not because Charlton were particularly good but because, as Derby's Jack Stamps unleashed a fierce shot which looked like securing victory 30 seconds from the end of normal time, the ball burst.

Before the game, the referee had joked about just such an embarrassment occurring – and claimed the odds were a million to one against. Ironically, it happened again the following year, when Charlton beat Burnley 1-0.

FA Cup *factfile*

Derby County have appeared in four finals, winning just the once in 1946 in their last appearance. Their first appearance was a 3-1 defeat by Nottingham Forest in 1898.

Charlton Athletic have appeared in two finals; their sole victory came in 1947, 1-0 v Burnley.

The Derby County team carry their captain Jack Nicholas on a lap of honour around Wembley

And Smith must score!

Brighton 2 Manchester United 2 1983

Brighton, already doomed to relegation, had played out of their skins in the FA Cup Final and found themselves level at 2-2 with mighty Manchester United, with 20 seconds of extra time remaining. Then suddenly Brighton's Gordon Smith found himself clean through with just the goalkeeper to beat – he couldn't miss.

"And Smith must score!" came the famous cry from commentator John Motson. Smith missed. Brighton lost the replay 4-0. The club itself plunged two divisions. Gordon Smith now runs a guest house near Falkirk.

Left: Brighton players congratulate Gary Stevens on scoring a last-gasp equaliser. With 20 seconds remaining, Gordon Smith – who had given Brighton the lead after 14 minutes – then had a chance to win the FA Cup. It was to be a costly miss. Manchester United (above) kept Brighton to a 1-1 draw with a goal by Frank Stapleton, and then five days later the Manchester millionaires won the replay 4-0. Earlier in the season, in the fifth round, Brighton had beaten mighty Liverpool at Anfield

FA Cup *factfile*

The 1983 Cup Final was Brighton's only appearance in the final, whereas Manchester United are the most successful FA Cup team with 15 final appearances and 10 victories. Their last victory was in 1999, 2-0 over Newcastle United; their first appearance came in 1909, a 1-0 win over Bristol City.

16

Saint Bobby

Southampton 1 Manchester United 0 1976

Three years after Sunderland's dramatic victory over favourites Leeds in the FA Cup, mighty Manchester United found themselves up against Southampton of Division Two. Once again, an upset was in the offing. Having kept United frustrated for the first half, Lawrie McMenemy's side broke clear shortly into the second as Mick Channon fed the ball to Bobby Stokes. From outside the penalty area, Stokes hit the ball low and hard. United keeper Alex Stepney dived, but the ball bobbled over his outstretched arm and into the corner of the net to secure a famous victory for the underdogs.

Alex Stepney dives in vain to save Bobby Stokes's shot. This single goal was enough to give Southampton a dramatic and historic victory

FA Cup *factfile*

Southampton have appeared in three FA Cup Finals, the last being their only victory in 1976. Their first appearance was a 4-0 defeat by Bury in 1900. The second was a 2-1 defeat two years later by Sheffield United.

Record-breaking Roberto

Chelsea 2 Middlesbrough 0 1997

18

Boro had high hopes of overturning the proud peacocks of Stamford Bridge in the FA Cup Final – but they were blown out of the water within a minute of the kick-off. Italian Roberto Di Matteo picked up the ball inside the Boro half, ran unimpeded towards the opposition goal, and unleashed a

Roberto Di Matteo scores the fastest FA Cup Final goal in history for Chelsea against Middlesbrough

right-foot screamer that flew into the back of the net. Timed at just 42 seconds, it was the fastest ever goal in a Final – and for Boro, there was no way back.

FA Cup *factfile*

Middlesbrough's only appearance came in 1997. **Chelsea** have appeared in 5 finals with 2 victories, the last being in 1997. The first appearance was a 3-0 defeat by Sheffield United in 1915.

Moran woe

Manchester United 1 Everton 0 1985

Referee Peter Willis dismisses Kevin Moran

When David Beckham made the lonely walk to the tunnel after his World Cup sending-off, Kevin Moran knew exactly how he was feeling. Moran remains the only man ever to be red-carded in an FA Cup Final. In the 1985 Wembley showpiece, Moran clipped Everton midfielder Peter Reid when he was the last defender – even though he was some 40 yards away from goal. Referee Peter Willis gave Moran his marching orders ... and until Beckham's dismissal against Argentina, it was probably the most infamous red card in English football history.

> *"If Everton were playing at the bottom of the garden, I'd pull the curtains."*
> Bill Shankly, former Liverpool manager

FA Cup *factfile*

Everton have appeared in 12 finals, winning five. Their last win was against Manchester United, 1-0 in 1995. Their first appearance was a 1-0 defeat by Wolves in 1893. Everton have also appeared in the most semi-finals, 23; Manchester United are second on 22.

Taking the p***

Leeds 7 Southampton 0 1972

Leeds *factfile*

Leeds United have won the Football League on three occasions, in 1968-69, 1973-74 and 1991-92. Their opponents that day, **Southampton**, have yet to top the League — their highest finish came in 1984, in 2nd place.

There is winning, winning in style, and then winning like Don Revie's Leeds United in this League match against hapless Southampton at Elland Road. Not only did they plant seven goals past the Saints, they then proceeded to completely remove the michael by playing extended keep-ball, to the joy of the jeering home crowd.

Leeds made 25 passes while Southampton's ragged side chased shadows. Unfortunately for them, the *Match of the Day* cameras were there to record every embarrassing pass for posterity.

Ruthless: Don Revie's mighty Leeds side of the early 1970s, from left — Billy Bremner, David Harvey, Paul Reaney, John Giles, Norman Hunter, Trevor Cherry, Joe Jordan, Gordon McQueen, Peter Lorimer, Paul Madeley, Allan Clarke and substitute Terry Yorath

Famous last words

Scotland 0 Costa Rica 1 1990

21

'We have nothing to fear from Costa Rica,' said a confident Scotland manager Andy Roxburgh on the eve of his side's first match in Italia 90. After 49 minutes, a neat back-heel by Claudio Jara fell invitingly for Juan Cayasso, who gratefully lifted the ball over the sprawling Jim Leighton. By beating the Scots, Costa Rica became the first Central American team to win a World Cup match in Europe.

Costa Rica celebrate Juan Cayasso's goal that condemned Scotland to a 1-0 defeat and an early exit from the 1990 World Cup. Both Group C teams went on to beat Sweden, and so it was Costa Rica who went through with Brazil to the second round

King Dennis

Holland 2 Argentina 1 1998

Unlike previous World Cup encounters between these two sides, the 1998 quarter-final in Marseille was a drab affair. With the score at 1-1, both teams appeared to be happy to go to extra time and then penalties.

However, as Brian Clough said, it only takes a second to score a goal – and although we had to wait until almost the very last one of this game for the winner, it was well worth it.

Frank de Boer's 40-yard pass upfield towards the isolated figure of Dennis Bergkamp was hopeful, to say the least. But, with a magical first touch, the Dutch master controlled the ball and, in almost his next stride, curled it perfectly out of the goalkeeper's reach and into the corner of the net.

Holland v Argentina *factfile*

Holland's record v Argentina

Played	Won	Drawn	Lost	Goals For	Goals Against
6	3	2	1	12	6

Biggest victory: 4-0, Gelsen Kirchen, 26.6.74
Biggest defeat: 3-1, Buenos Aires, 25.6.78

Arsenal and Holland hero Dennis Bergkamp scores the dramatic late winner against Argentina in the 1998 World Cup quarter-finals in Marseille

Weah beats them all

AC Milan 2 Verona 0 1996

Milan striker George Weah is renowned for his eye for goal. On this occasion, a Serie A match in the San Siro, he spotted the opportunity while on his own six-yard line. Lurking deep inside his own penalty area for a Verona corner, Weah picked up a bobbling loose header and, with no one up front, set off on a weaving run in which the ball appeared to be glued to his foot.

23

> *"I'm not giving away any secrets like that (the team line-up) to Milan. If I had my way, I wouldn't even tell them the time of the kick-off."*
> Bill Shankly

In true *Roy of the Rovers* style, the lanky Liberian proceeded to dribble his way 90 yards through the entire Verona team before firing past the keeper.

Weah *factfile*

In 1995, George Weah was voted the World Footballer of the Year, European Footballer of the Year and African Footballer of the Year. He is the only player ever to hold these honours simultaneously.

George Weah — the Liberia and AC Milan striker — shows off the dribbling skills that went into his wonder goal against Verona in Italy's Serie A

The Lawman's harsh sentence

Manchester United 0 Manchester City 1 1974

They called him the Lawman, and on this occasion Denis Law condemned his former club Manchester United to the Second Division with the very last bullet in his gun.

Having been an Old Trafford idol before his transfer across town to Maine Road, Law must have hoped to have returned to his former haunt in happier circumstances than these.

United, shorn of so many of their great stars, were almost through the trapdoor, and a defeat meant the drop. Law, in his final game,

proved he still had a few tricks up his sleeve when an impulsive, impudent back heel sent the ball into the back of the United net for a 1-0 City victory – celebrated deliriously by City's fans, but with decidedly mixed feelings by Law, who was immediately substituted and never played again. Later he said: "I went home and shed tears. I have never regretted scoring, but I have always wished the goal hadn't been so important or ironic."

League *factfile*

Manchester United have won the championship 12 times, the first being in 1907-08, the last in 1998-99.

Manchester City have won it twice, in 1936-37 and in 1967-68, the same season United won the European Cup.

Denis the menace: A United hero for many years, Law condemned his old club to relegation in the last game of his career

> "Matt Busby always believed Manchester United would be one of the greatest clubs in the world. He was the eternal optimist. In 1968 he still hoped Glenn Miller was just missing."
>
> Pat Crerand

The Carlos free kick

Brazil 1 France 0 1997

As a precursor to the World Cup the following year, Le Tournoi – a knockout between France, England, Brazil and Italy – was proving something of a damp squib, until Brazilian right back Roberto Carlos brought it to life in sensational fashion.

Awarded a free-kick some 30 yards out, the stocky defender, proud owner of surely the biggest thighs in football, began his cricket-style run-up. Struck with the outside of Roberto Carlos's left boot, the ball fired off to the left of the French defensive wall.

A photographer standing well to the left of the goal saw the ball fizzing towards him and began to take evasive action. Between the sticks, balding French goalkeeper Fabien Barthez reasoned that the shot was powerful, but going well wide of his left post.

He was wrong. The ball began to curve round at an almost unbelievable angle, at

85 mph, and far too late for the bemused Barthez to do anything to prevent it going into the back of the net off a post. As players and spectators gasped in astonishment, only the prostrate photographer felt more embarrassed than the goalkeeper.

"You know, the Brazilians aren't as good as they used to be, or as they are now."
Kenny Dalglish

Roberto Carlos's amazingly fast, swerving, dipping free-kick against France caused a bit of a sensation in 1997

Brilliant Beckham

Wimbledon 0 Manchester United 3 1996

Long before Posh weddings and sarongs, David Beckham was happiest grabbing the headlines with his on-the-pitch activities. United were 2-0 up and coasting to an opening day victory against hapless Wimbledon when Becks received the ball ten yards inside his own half near the right touchline. Looking up, he noticed that Neil Sullivan, the Dons keeper, was off his line, and launched a speculative lob.

The ball seemed to hang in the air for an eternity, although it was travelling at sufficient speed to catch Sullivan unawares and beat him to the back of the net for a stunning individual goal.

Up in the commentary box, John Motson nearly fell off the gantry with excitement.

Beckham *factfile*

Born: 2.5.75, Leytonstone, England
Height: 180 cm   **Weight:** 71kg
Position: Midfield
Games: 183   **Goals:** 41
Clubs: Manchester United
First-team debut: v Brighton (Coca-Cola Cup) 23.9.92
League debut: v Leeds Utd 2.4.95
International appearances/Goals: 24/1

Superstar: David Beckham of Manchester United and England, the man who has it all. He also has one of the greatest long-range goals of all time to his credit

26

Kung Fu Cantona

Crystal Palace 1 Manchester United 2 1995

C an it really be nearly five years since Monsieur Eric Cantona's infamous brand of martial arts brought the 'beautiful game' into such riotous disrepute? During a niggly match at Selhurst Park, United figurehead Cantona had just been sent off for kicking Palace defender Richard Shaw.

27 As he stalked along the touchline to the tunnel, an overweight thug named Matthew Simmons decided he would add his own verdict to the proceedings by casting aspersions upon Eric's mum back home in France. Le red mist descended, and Cantona launched himself Bruce Lee style – and with studs very much raised – at the Palace fan.

Cantona was sentenced to two weeks' imprisonment at Croydon Magistrates' Court, later commuted to 120 hours community service. Simmons was fined £500 pie money for threatening behaviour.

Eric told the media: "When the seagulls follow the trawler, it is because they think the fishes are going to be thrown into the sea."

"The first wasn't a foul, so I thought, if they want a foul I'll give them a foul."
Eric Cantona
explains his second sending-off in consecutive games at Arsenal, 1994

Cantona *factfile*

Born: 24.5.66, Nîmes, France
Height: 188cm
Weight: 88kg
Position: Centre forward
Clubs: Auxerre, Martigues, Marseille, Bordeaux, Montpellier, Nîmes, Leeds United, Manchester United
International appearances: 39
International goals: 19

What an entertainer...Eric Cantona put on a great show at Selhurst Park in January 1995 when, after being sent off, he reacted to the jeering crowd by launching a kung-fu style kick at one of the main offenders

Tears of a clown

England 1 West Germany 1 1990

You could see it coming, you were screaming at him not to do it, that it wasn't necessary – but you knew at the same time there was a sad inevitability about Paul Gascoigne getting booked for a rash challenge in this World Cup semi-final, thereby ruling himself out of the Final.

Gazza duly obliged, with a late tackle on the innocuous Thomas

> *"If history is going to repeat itself, I should think we can expect the same again."*
>
> Terry Venables

Berthold. To his credit, Gascoigne played his heart out until the final whistle. Then, as the two sides prepared for penalties, the Geordie boy sealed his place in football immortality by bursting into inconsolable tears.

"He's lost it," Gary Lineker had indicated to the bench. He was right – but Gazza also gained the respect of the world that sultry Turin night.

Gazza *factfile*

Born: 27.5.67,
Gateshead, England
Height: 179cm   **Weight:** 79kg
Position: Central midfield
Clubs: Newcastle United, Tottenham, Lazio, Glasgow Rangers, Middlesbrough
International appearances: 57
International goals: 10

Above: The German team celebrate on the pitch after winning the penalty shoot-out against England. Right: Paul Gascoigne loses it and bursts into tears, a sight that gained him thousands of fans

28

Boy's Owen

Argentina 2 England 2 1998

Finally heeding the pleas of the English fans who had watched their side stumble and stutter into the World Cup second round, manager Glenn Hoddle decided to give Liverpool's *wunderkind* Michael Qwen his head against Argentina in St-Etienne. The youngster did not let him down. In fact, in scoring probably the goal of the tournament, he made the stubborn Hoddle look positively stupid.

Picking up a pass from David Beckham on halfway, Owen showed blistering pace to outstrip two Argie defenders on his way to the penalty area. Veering right in order to get round a third, Owen beat his own player, the lurking Paul Scholes, to the ball before cracking it majestically into the top corner of the net. Sadly, Owen's work was to be in vain...

29

Using his pace to get past the Argentine defenders, Owen heads for goal before cracking an unstoppable shot

Owen *factfile*

Born: 14.12.79, Chester, England
Height: 176cm
Weight: 70kg
Position: Forward
Clubs: Liverpool
International appearances: 11
Goals: 4

Beckham sees red
Argentina 2 England 2 1998

David Beckham, who had covered himself in glory with a trademark thunderbolt free-kick against Colombia, covered himself in something far more unpleasant and long-lasting a few minutes into the second half of the match.

With the score at 2-2, England had been playing some of their best football

> *"I hear Glenn Hoddle has found God. That must have been one hell of a pass."*
> Jasper Carrott

of the tournament. Beckham, along with his Manchester United pal Paul Scholes, had zipped up the midfield and there was real expectancy that a win could be on the cards.

Then, disaster. Fouled by Diego Simeone on halfway, Beckham, lying face-down on the ground, reacted with a petulant flick of his red boot. Simeone in turn went down as if shot with a Magnum.

There was a stomach-churning moment of disbelief as the England midfielder was hauled across to the referee – then a nation-wide head-in-hands as the red card was brandished.

Although England fought a brave rear-guard action with ten men and eventually lost on penalties, Beckham would get the blame for a disappointingly early World Cup exit.

Turning point: After a pointless act of retaliation, David Beckham is given his marching orders

England v Argentina *factfile*

England's record v Argentina

Played	Won	Drawn	Lost	Goals For	Goals Against
11	4	5	2	17	13

Biggest victories: 3-1, Wembley, 13.5.80 and Racagua, Chile, 2.6.62
Biggest defeat: 2-1, Mexico City, 22.6.86

England red cards *factfile*

Allan Mullery	v Yugoslavia, Florence, 5.6.68
Alan Ball	v Poland, Chorzow, 6.6.73
Trevor Cherry	v Argentina, Buenos Aires, 12.6.77
Ray Wilkins	v Morocco, Monterrey, 6.6.86
David Beckham	v Argentina, Saint-Etienno, 30.6.98
Paul Ince	v Sweden, Stockholm, 5.9.98
Paul Scholes	v Sweden, London, 5.6.99

They think it's all over
England 4 West Germany 2 1966

31

There were indeed some people on the pitch – but they were running the opposite way to England striker Geoff Hurst as, in the dying seconds of extra time, he latched on to Bobby Moore's exquisite pass. With the very last of his energy, and with a German defender in tow, Hurst made it to the edge of the penalty area before unleashing an absolute screamer of a left-foot shot into the top corner of Tilkowski's net.

Later, Hurst admitted he had been trying to smash it out of the ground. Instead, he

"...it is now!" The 1966 World Cup Final – England's famous fourth goal in a 4-2 win, completing a hat-trick for Hurst and sealing a deserved victory

scored the goal which symbolised England's historic World Cup Final win.

The hand of God
Argentina 2 England 1 1986

Remember Steve Hodge? England's unspectacular midfielder did little of any note during the 1986 Mexico World Cup, yet he was indirectly responsible for one of the most controversial goals in the history of the game. For it was Hodge's sliced clearance kick back into his own penalty area that set up the one-on-one chase for the ball between the respective captains Diego Maradona and Peter Shilton in this unforgettable quarter-final.

As the ball bounced on the hard Azteca stadium turf, Shilton, towering over the diminutive Argentine, was clear favourite to get there first. Then, with a prodigious leap, Maradona punched the ball from Shilton's extended glove with his left hand and into the empty net. Uproar ensued, and quite rightly so.

Tunisian referee Ali Ben Nasser gave the goal. Maradona enigmatically described the incident later as "the hand of God". But perhaps he might have been feeling slightly guilty, because four minutes later he produced a truly divine moment that had even begrudging England fans admitting that the cheating little so-and-so was not of this planet.

A shock for Shilton as the shortest man on the pitch jumps high enough to 'head' the ball above the England goalkeeper's hands

The feet of God

Argentina 2 England 1 1986

33

Maradona on his way to beating Kenny Sansom and Terry Butcher before scoring Argentina's second goal

Diego Maradona receives congratulations from his team-mates after his brilliant goal. Look, no hands...

Picking the ball up just inside his own half on the right, Maradona began a full-blooded hurtle at the England defence. Yet amid all the power, there was almost unbelievable artistry as the stocky striker wove an intricate, high-speed pattern that shook off first Gary Stevens, then Terry Butcher, then Terry Fenwick, then Butcher again before finally the out-rushing

"With Maradona, even Arsenal would have won it."

Bobby Robson
sums up the 1986 World Cup

goalkeeper Peter Shilton was left for dead by a delicate chip that left the ball nestling in the back of the net.

"You have to say that was magnificent," gasped commentator Barry Davies. And you had to agree with him.

The feet of God, Part two

Argentina 2 Belgium 0 1986

As if to prove that his solo supreme against England was no fluke, Maradona did it again against Belgium in the semi-final. The Belgians, backs to the wall, had defended gamely. But in the 51st minute Maradona broke them with a well-taken goal and then, in the 63rd minute, unpicked their packed defence with breathtaking close control.

"I don't think there is anybody bigger or smaller than Maradona."

Kevin Keegan

Again, barrel-chested, the Argentinian captain ran straight into the heart of the opposition penalty area. Again, he skipped his way through half a dozen opponents.

And again, he had the presence of mind and the subtlety of footwork to round the keeper – in this case Belgium's Jean-Marie Pfaff – before burying the ball into the net.

Six Belgians against Diego Maradona? Not good odds – as the Belgians discovered when Argentina's pocket battleship ripped through their defences to score another out-of-this-world goal. Maradona's name was written on the World Cup in 1986, and Argentina duly won a pulsating Final against West Germany 3-2

34

A Maradona cocktail

Argentina 4 Greece 0 1994

35

Crazy guy: Maradona, who later trained with disgraced Olympic sprinter Ben Johnson, had taken five banned drugs

After years in the drug-addled wilderness, Maradona returned to the world stage at Boston's Foxboro Stadium in this World Cup Group D match against the lowly Greeks. The result, 4-0, was never in doubt. The revelation was Maradona. After being written off, he produced a sublime display, bursting with stamina and energy, that culminated in his 60th-minute goal and the extraordinary, twisted, almost inhuman face he pulled directly at one of the pitch-side cameras.

Slightly taken-aback observers put this display down to the fact Maradona was pumped up for the game. But when he produced a similarly charged performance in his next match against the Nigerians, suspicions were first voiced then confirmed when Maradona's urine was found to contain a cocktail of five illegal drugs.

> "I have even taken drugs twenty minutes before a match.
> It was a few years ago and I paid the price. I started the match on speed and ended it on crutches."
>
> Martin Neil, captain of Berwick Rangers, describes his experiences in the Scottish Third Division

The Cruyff turn

Holland 0 Sweden 0 1974

That Holland's Johan Cruyff was the world's finest player in 1974 was not the issue. Neither was the fact that he was the most frustratingly enigmatic. He had a tendency to go AWOL for long periods during a game, then suddenly light up the skies with a moment of pure genius.

Such was the case in the World Cup game against Sweden in Dortmund. The match ended 0-0, but is remembered for the moment in the first half when the great man unveiled the now legendary "Cruyff turn".

Stuck on the edge of the penalty area, and with Swedish defender Jan Olsson bearing down on him, Cruyff shaped to cross. Yet even as Olsson lunged, Cruyff wrapped his foot round the ball and almost twisted inside out in order to flick the ball behind himself and was suddenly galloping to the byline with the defender sprawled on his backside. The subsequent cross, with the outside of the foot, was perfect. Pity the chance was missed.

36

Holland v Sweden *factfile*					
Holland's record v Sweden					
Played	Won	Drawn	Lost	Goals For	Goals Against
18	8	3	7	33	40

Biggest victory: 5-1, Stockholm, 4.9.74
Biggest defeat: 6-1, Stockholm, 19.5.54

Cruyffed! The Dutchman was one of football's great mavericks, with endless new ways to embarrass opponents

Sensational Salas
England 0 Chile 2 1998

A friendly match this might have been – but Chilean frontman Marcelo Salas took it as an opportunity to display his majestic skills before an amazed Wembley crowd.

As ever with the lesser-known countries of South America, many in the crowd – and, indeed, in the newspapers – had been expecting an easy victory for Kevin Keegan's team. Salas had other ideas...

Latching on to a 40-yard pass, Salas languidly cushioned the ball on his thigh before thrashing it unstoppably into the back of Nigel Martyn's net from outside the penalty area.

England v Chile *factfile*

England's record v Chile

Played	Won	Drawn	Lost	Goals For	Goals Against
5	2	2	1	4	3

Biggest victory: 2-0, Rio de Janeiro, 25.6.50
Biggest defeat: 2-0, Wembley, 11.2.98

Sweet as Salas: The Chilean striker sent England spinning to defeat with a fantastic goal in a friendly at Wembley before the World Cup Finals

What's he doing there?

Real Madrid 3 Manchester Utd 4 (agg) 1968

38

Manager Sir Matt Busby enjoys victory with his United team

It was George Best who most memorably summed up United's unforgettable winning goal in the European Cup semi-final in front of 90,000 screaming fans in Madrid. With the score 3-3 on aggregate and 12 minutes left, the willowy Best received the ball from Paddy Crerand's throw-in and, shimmying past the Spanish defence, made it to the byeline. Looking up, Best saw only a red shirt following him into the penalty area.

"Had I known it was Bill Foulkes, there is no way I would have passed to him," Best later remarked. Foulkes, United's central defender who was built like a brick outhouse, had for some reason charged upfield and was as surprised as anyone to receive Best's inch-perfect pass just inside the penalty area.

As ace goalscorers Best and Bobby Charlton looked on, Foulkes struck the ball perfectly first time into the back of the net to secure a famous victory for United. "To this day I don't know what I was doing there," Foulkes said. "It could only have been divine inspiration."

Platt's late late show

Belgium 0 England 1 1990

39

David Platt celebrates after scoring a sensational late winner against Belgium in Bologna

England joy and jubilation means that Platt is buried under his team-mates

After recovering from the dodgiest of starts, England, it seemed, were back on track for World Cup glory with Paul Gascoigne, Gary Lineker and Chris Waddle at last firing on all cylinders. Against Belgium in the second round, the shaky house of cards once again seemed about to topple with the score goalless and the match heading towards the lottery of penalties.

In the dying seconds of extra time, Gascoigne launched a long, dipping free-kick into the heart of the Belgian defence. Platt watched it looping over his shoulder and, bending his body, volleyed it across himself and into the net.

England v Belgium *factfile*

England's record v Belgium

Played	Won	Drawn	Lost	Goals For	Goals Against
19	13	5	1	67	24

Biggest victory: 9-1, Brussels, 11.5.27
Biggest defeat: 3-2, Brussels, 9.5.36

Porterfield — One-nil!

Leeds 0 Sunderland 1 1973

Sunderland of the Second Division had been widely expected to be at least three goals down by the time they took a decisive 1-0 lead over Don Revie's mighty Leeds in the 1973 Cup Final. The goal came from a corner, which the Tykes failed to clear. The ball bounced up and Sunderland's Ian Porterfield cracked it right-footed into the back of the net. It was to be one of the great FA Cup upsets of all time.

Ian Porterfield, far right, thunders in an unstoppable shot to clinch Sunderland's historic win in the 1973 FA Cup Final, as the supposedly impregnable Leeds United defence look on in disbelief. It was one of Wembley's greatest upsets

Monty's double save
Leeds 0 Sunderland 1 1973

The fact that Sunderland boss Bob Stokoe ran first to Jim Montgomery rather than goalscorer Ian Porterfield on the final whistle is an indication of the part his goalkeeper played in the Wearsiders' historic FA Cup Final win. Backs to the wall ever since scoring their shock goal, Sunderland looked bound to crack at any minute. Trevor Cherry must have thought he'd equalised when, in the second half he smashed in a close-range shot. Montgomery somehow managed to parry it.

The ball rolled straight to the feet of Peter Lorimer. "And Lorimer makes it one each!" screamed David Coleman as the Scottish striker leathered the ball from no more than six yards.

But Coleman and everyone else in the ground was wrong, as Monty astonishingly pulled off a reaction save and pushed the ball up and over the bar.

Right. Bobby Kerr is held aloft by his team-mates. Keeper Jim Montgomery wears the FA Cup lid as a hat

A star is born

Brazil 1 Wales 0

1958

42

Wales? In a World Cup quarter-final? Yes, it's true that in Sweden in 1958 the Welsh – inspired by John Charles and Ivor Allchurch – proudly won their way through to the last eight.

They might have gone further had they not faced Brazil, and in particular their brilliant young star, Pele.

Aged just 17, Pele had already been an international for a year. This was his first World Cup, and against the hapless Welsh he scored his first World Cup goal. And what a cracker it was.

Taking Didi's headed pass on his chest, Pele flicked it away from the defender before it bounced, then shot hard from eight yards. Williams' vain attempt to block the shot merely slowed it on its way in.

Barnes' Brazilian touch

Brazil 0 England 2

1984

43

It was a goal any Brazilian would have been proud to have scored. England's John Barnes picked up the ball on the left of midfield and set off on a mazy, diagonal run which took him into the heart of the Brazil penalty area and past four sprawling defenders before sliding

> *"On those performances I reckon we would have taken Brazil."*
>
> Neil Ruddock on Liverpool's 100 per cent start to the 1994-95 season

the ball coolly into the back of the net. Samba soccer indeed. Even though it was a friendly match, it was an amazing feat. Barnes was just 20 at the time – and, in a long, distinguished career, would never again reach the heights of that glorious night.

Brazil 0 England 2, at the Maracana Stadium: John Barnes sets off on his mesmeric run for goal

Foul free-kick
Coventry 1 Everton 1
1974

The whistle sounded: free-kick to Coventry City. Twenty yards out, Willie Carr exchanged a knowing look with his striking partner Ernie Hunt. They had discussed the move in the bar many times, practised it on the training pitch even more. Now it was time to try it out for real, in the glare of a First Division match.

Standing directly over the ball, Carr flicked the ball backwards and upwards with his heels. As the Everton wall watched with bemusement, Hunt caught the ball perfectly on the volley and smashed it into the net. The goal stood – although almost immediately afterwards, the Football Association mandarins agreed that that ploy would be banned. Still, it hasn't stopped everyone from attempting it.

"I know this is a sad occasion but I think Dixie would be amazed to know that even in death he could draw a bigger crowd than Everton can on a Saturday afternoon."
Bill Shankly at Dixie Dean's funeral

Simply the best of Brazil

Brazil 4 Italy 1 1970

In beating Italy 4-1 in the 1970 World Cup Final in Mexico's Azteca Stadium, Brazil merely confirmed what everyone had realised during the course of the tournament – that they were by far and away the greatest football team of all time. But to sum up just how great they were, there is no better example than their fourth goal, scored by Carlos Alberto.

It began with Clodoaldo bringing the ball almost casually out of his own defence, ghosting past the Italians as if they weren't there. Next, the ball was with Jairzinho who took and turned in just one movement before finding Pele lurking on the edge of the penalty area. As the blue shirts gathered around him, Pele seemed to sense the runaway train steaming up on the right flank. A lazy, yet marvellously inch-perfect stroke of the ball placed it directly in the stride of defender Carlos Alberto, who struck it with such power and accuracy it went like a missile straight into the corner of the net and would no doubt have continued for another 100 yards at the same speed.

Pele turns away after scoring Brazil's first goal against Italy in the 1970 World Cup Final

So nearly perfection

Brazil 3 Uruguay 1

1970

What a goal it would have been. But even though Pele missed, his moment of genius in this World Cup semi-final against South American rivals Uruguay was good enough to enter any hall of fame.

Latching on to a long through ball from Tostao, Pele was one-on-one with keeper Mazurkiewicz. Rather than dribble round him, the Brazilian allowed the ball to go through his legs, leaving the keeper sprawled on the ground. Racing round to collect the ball again, Pele swivelled and fired in a shot that rolled agonisingly past the far post.

Just as well. According to one Brazilian observer, if Pele had scored then all football should be abandoned because there would be nothing left to achieve.

Green and white glory

Inter Milan 1 Celtic 2 1967

Long before Manchester United's heroics in Barcelona, the first British club to win the European Cup were Celtic. Their victory over Italy's Inter was, in many respects, a greater achievement than United's. Inter were the masters of catenaccio – the ability to score a goal and then effectively stifle the game with chained defence.

47

When they went a goal up after just seven minutes in Lisbon, few gave the Glasgow club a chance of even attempting an equaliser. Yet Inter were to be subjected to an extraordinary, hour-long barrage of attacking football by the Scots which left their famed defence first rocking, then burst apart.

First, Gemmell equalised with a thunderous 25-yard shot. Then, with five minutes to go, a cross shot from Murdoch was diverted into the Inter net by Chalmers for a famous victory.

Billy McNeill receives the European Cup from the president of Portugal after Celtic win 2-1 in Lisbon

Viva Villa

Tottenham 3 Manchester City 1 1981

Having been substituted in the drawn FA Cup Final after an ineffective display, Spurs' bearded Argentine Ricky Villa clearly felt he had a point to make. Sure enough, his goal in the replay stands alongside any of the Wembley greats. Receiving the ball just outside the Manchester City penalty area, Villa set off on a mazy, weaving run in which he beat Tommy Caton three times, as well as Ray Ransom and Nicy Reid, before sliding the ball into the net through a forest of legs. It was a rare moment of glory for Villa, who never emulated the success of his Argentine colleague Ossie Ardiles. Indeed that season Villa scored just two goals in 29 league starts for Spurs. But his FA Cup Final goal was the best ever.

> *"And I suppose Spurs are nearer to being out of the FA Cup now than any other time since the first half of this season, when they weren't ever in it anyway."*
> John Motson

At last Ricky Villa gets his hands on the FA Cup

Ricky Villa doesn't know where to run after scoring his sensational goal

The Dons do Liverpool

Wimbledon 1 Liverpool 0 1988

Liverpool were in their pomp in 1988 – but they were undone in the FA Cup Final by Wimbledon's relentless long-ball game, a headed goal by Lawrie Sanchez, and by David Beasant's penalty save – the first ever in a Wembley Cup Final.

Until that fateful day, Liverpool's John Aldridge had been on deadly spot-kick form, having scored eleven out of eleven during that season. Ironically, it was his penalty expertise that was to prove his undoing. Prior to the Final, Beasant had bought himself a video recorder and watched re-runs of every penalty Aldridge had taken. As the Liverpool striker lined up, Beasant therefore knew that Aldridge always hit it to the keeper's left.

Sure enough, Aldridge hit it to the keeper's left and Beasant saved it. Wimbledon won the Cup and Beasant was rewarded shortly after with a £1 million transfer to Newcastle United.

49

Top: Beasant's crucial penalty save.
Right: The Wimbledon team celebrate

Lawrie Sanchez's headed goal decided the Final

Robbo strikes early
England 3 France 1 1982

50

Back in the World Cup finals after 12 years of unmitigated qualification failure, England kicked off in Spain '82 with a group match in Bilbao against France. But with Trevor Brooking and Kevin Keegan injured, few expected a side containing the likes of Paul Mariner, Graham Rix and Mick Mills to do much damage to a French side which boasted such luminaries as Giresse, Platini and Tigana.

But we calculated without Bryan Robson.

Indeed, it took Robson just 27 seconds to score. From Steve Coppell's throw-in on the right, a back-header by Terry Butcher found the Manchester United midfielder completely unmarked in the penalty area. With a spectacular left-foot volley, Robson hammered the ball past French keeper Ettori to claim the quickest goal in World Cup history.

England won 3-1, and cruised into the next play-off round, where they drew with Spain and West Germany, and so went out unbeaten.

Bryan Robson opens the scoring after 27 seconds

England v France *factfile*

England's record v France

Played	Won	Drawn	Lost	Goals For	Goals Against
24	16	3	5	63	30

Biggest victory: 6-0, Paris, 26.5.27
Biggest defeat: 5-2, Paris, 14.5.31

What a match
Italy 3 Brazil 2 1982

One of the great World Cup matches saw Italy and Brazil fight tooth and nail for a place in the semi-finals. Brazil, with Socrates, Junior, Zico and Eder lighting up the tournament, needed just a draw. But Italy were about to play the game of their lives – and they had Paolo Rossi up front.

Five minutes had passed when Rossi nodded home Antonio Cabrini's cross to open the scoring.

But within 10 minutes the Brazilians were level, Zico's marvellous back-heeled turn setting up a chance for Socrates, which the elegant midfielder hammered past Dino Zoff.

Even the Italian fans assumed the inevitable Brazilian victory would follow – but then a dreadful blunder by Cerezo gifted a chance to Rossi, who raced away and shot straight through keeper Waldir Peres.

In the second half, Rossi should have wrapped it up

when Graziani rolled the ball across the six-yard area only for Rossi to blaze it over the bar from point-blank range.

The error was compounded within minutes when Junior fed Falcao, who drove home an unstoppable shot to equalise. His face, contorted with delight, was to be one of the images of the tournament.

But joy turned to tears shortly afterwards with the final twist of this remarkable match.

On 74 minutes Marco Tardelli's weak shot turned into the perfect through-ball for the deadshot Rossi, who swivelled on the six-yard line to despatch a true predator's goal.

Still the drama continued. Antognoni had a perfectly good goal disallowed for offside.

Then, with two minutes left, the ageing Zoff produced a miraculous goal-line save from Oscar's header.

Paolo Rossi scored a hat-trick to secure a famous win against a strong Brazilian side

51

The best ever?
Hungary 4 Uruguay 2 (aet) 1954

The greatest international of all time? This 1954 World Cup semi-final takes the biscuit for many observers.

Hungary were a goal up after 12 minutes and Hidegkuti's marvellous diving header just after half-time made it 2-0 to the Magyars. But in heavy rain in Lausanne, Uruguay staged a brilliant recovery.

Hohberg pulled one back on 76 minutes and then the supremely talented Shiaffino scrambled home a dramatic equaliser with just three minutes left on the clock.

In extra time there was more drama as Hohberg hit the post, before two bullet-headers from Kocsis sealed victory for Hungary: a fitting end to a great game.

52

The Hungarian goalkeeper Roque Maspoli clears the ball with his fist, during the match against Uruguay in the 1954 World Cup semi-final, which took place in Berne, Switzerland

Supermac on song
England 5 Cyprus 0 1975

53

Malcolm Macdonald was one of the great strikers of the 1970s and a huge favourite with Newcastle United fans – it was just unfortunate that his best coincided with some of the national side's darkest days both in terms of performances, available talent, and selection policy.

"Mirandinha will have more shots this afternoon than both sides put together."
Malcolm Macdonald as commentator

Poor Cyprus – Supermac just couldn't stop scoring

Still, Supermac made a sensational impact on his England debut against an admittedly woeful Cyprus team at Wembley. England won 5-0, and Macdonald scored all five – a post-war record.

Radford's rocket

Hereford United 2 Newcastle United 1 1972

The Gallowgate End was expecting a goal feast when non-League Hereford United turned up at St James' Park in the FA Cup Third Round. Instead, they were shocked when the part-timers held the First Division side to a 2-2 draw. And if that was bad, then there was worse to come in the replay at Hereford's Edgar Street.

On a filthy day and on a pitch resembling a mudbath, Newcastle seemed to have overcome the home side's initial harrying when Malcolm Macdonald gave them the lead. Despite this, the non-Leaguers never gave up and, with just four minutes left, they scored one of the most unforgettable goals ever.

Ronnie Radford, a joiner by trade, picked up possession in the centre circle. Executing a one-two with team-mate Brian Owen, Radford made brief headway through the mud before unleashing a shot from more than 40 yards out. The ball fairly rocketed past Ian McFaul in the Newcastle goal, provoking a delighted pitch invasion. Stunned, Newcastle found themselves having to play out extra time.

The inevitable happened when Hereford's Ricky George clipped home the winner, ensuring legendary status for Hereford and ignominy for the Toon Army.

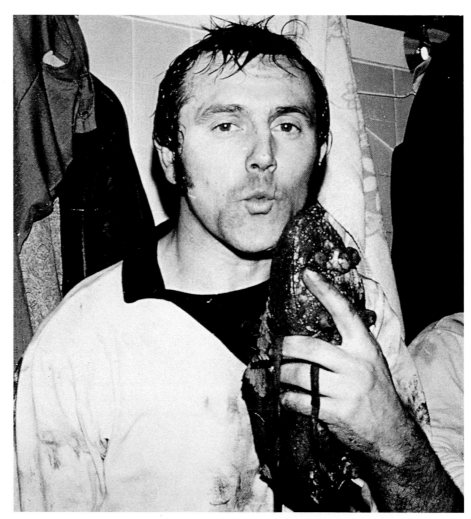

Ronnie Radford – a joiner by trade – kisses his boots after FA Cup glory with Hereford in 1972

Gazza blows away the Gunners

Tottenham Hotspur 1 Arsenal 0 1991

Fresh from his personal tears and triumphs during Italia 90, Paul Gascoigne had enjoyed his best ever season, sending the White Hart Lane faithful into raptures with his pace, skill and goals. The FA Cup semi-final against Arsenal at Wembley was about to put the icing on the cake.

Five minutes into the match, Arsenal's Anders Limpar sent Paul Stewart sprawling with an ill-timed tackle. From more than 30 yards, Gazza lined up the free kick and sent an explosive right-foot drive over the three-man Gunners' wall and straight into the top corner of the net.

A moment of utter silence then the great old stadium erupted in salute of one of the great free kicks.

Something special: Gazza goes to salute the crowd after scoring from 35 yards with an absolutely stunning free-kick

55

Gazza's moment of madness

Tottenham Hotspur 2 Nottingham Forest 1 1991

Paul Gascoigne's sensational strike against Arsenal had sent Tottenham Hotspur into the FA Cup Final. Ironically, not to say tragically, it was this game that provided the incident which was to knock the Geordie genius's career into tailspin. Psyched up out of all proportion, Gascoigne went looking for Forest players to tackle straight from the opening whistle.

56

He was warned almost immediately for a foot-up challenge, yet continued with his seemingly kamikaze mission. Observers began to wonder how long it would be until he got his marching orders.

Unfortunately, Gazza's eagerness was to have far more serious consequences.

As Forest's Gary Charles brought the ball out of defence, the Tottenham midfielder attempted a tackle. His right leg went across Charles's knees and both players collapsed in a heap.

Gascoigne's horrendous foot-up challenge on Gary Charles resulted in a long lay-off with a serious knee injury. Some would say he was never the same player

"The doctor at Lazio told me I should try drinking wine, because it would be good for me. When I did he had one look at me and said: 'You'd better go back on the beer'."
Paul Gascoigne

At first it was not obvious that Gazza was injured. Indeed for a couple of minutes he attempted to play on.

But when he finally fell to the ground clutching his knee, everyone realised that he was down and out. Stretchered from the pitch in tears, he was taken straight to a London hospital where surgeons immediately operated on his wrecked knee joint.

Although he would recover sufficiently to play, and eventually go to Italy on a long-planned transfer to Lazio, Gascoigne would never be the same player again.

A clanger by Clemence
Scotland 2 England 1 1976

It's 1-1 in the cauldron of Hampden Park in the Home International clash between the two bitter rivals Scotland and England. The ball comes to striker Kenny Dalglish on the edge of England's penalty area. Goalkeeper Ray Clemence braces himself for a Dalglish thunderbolt.

Instead, the Celtic striker scuffs the shot, sending it bobbling harmlessly along the turf. Clemence reaches down like a cricket fielder to collect the ball. The ball runs under his hands and through his legs and trickles into the net.

A 2-1 victory to Scotland and Clemence is the toast of Hampden.

57

Oops! Ray Clemence must have wished the ground would swallow him up after his disastrous mistake against Scotland

A Sprake nightmare
Liverpool 2 Leeds 1 1971

The name of Gary Sprake still provokes riotous laughter among a certain generation of football fans nearly 30 years after his goalkeeping gaffes made him a household name. Ironically, the Welshman was initially perceived as a keeper of brilliance. But in the 1970 FA Cup Final, Sprake let in a sitter against Chelsea and things just went pear-shaped from that moment on.

58

Of all Sprake's cock-ups, none was better than his effort in a League match against Liverpool at Anfield. Defending the Kop end, Leeds' Jack Charlton passed the ball back to Sprake. Sprake looked up and saw Paul Reaney calling for it on the touchline. Just as he was about to throw out, Sprake noticed the looming figure of Liverpool's John Toshack coming over to cover Reaney.

Changing his mind, Sprake checked his throw and turned away. But in doing so, he inadvertently hurled the greasy ball into his own net.

The ever-sharp Kop immediately began a joyous rendition of the current pop song *Careless Hands* – a hit which would remain Sprake's anthem until he retired.

Gary Sprake will unfortunately always be remembered for throwing the ball into his own net against Liverpool in a League match

England shame
USA 1 England 0 1950

Upsets don't come much bigger than this in the 1950 World Cup in Brazil. England were not only expected to win, the prospect of them losing to the United States was simply out of the question. Yet the team, which included Stan Mortensen, Tom Finney and future World Cup-winning boss Alf Ramsey, was about to set a precedent for big-time flops that would become a part of English football history.

The match was played in a small stadium in Belo Horizonte on a bumpy pitch. England immediately set up camp in the USA half. They hit the post, shot over the bar and did everything but score. Surely a goal was only a matter of time. And indeed it was.

Eight minutes before half-time, a hopeful shot by the USA's Bahr was nodded home by striker Gaetens. 1-0. And that was how it remained as, in the second half, England were given the first of many lessons in not underestimating lowly opposition.

England v USA *factfile*

England's record v USA

Played	Won	Drawn	Lost	Goals For	Goals Against
7	5	0	2	31	7

Biggest victory: 10-0, New York, 27.5.37
Biggest defeat: 2-0, Foxboro, Mass, 9.6.93

The England football team arrive back at Heathrow Airport from Rio after their World Cup failure.
Standing at the bottom of the aeroplane steps are, from left to right and ascending: Ted Ditchburn (behind Mullen), Roy Bentley, Willie Watson, Stan Mortensen, Bert Williams, Walter Winterbottom (manager), Alf Ramsey, Tailor, Jackie Milburn, Stanley Matthews, Wilf Mannion, Tom Finney, Scott, Hughes and Cockburn

Gray's play-off disaster

Sunderland 4 Charlton Athletic 4 (Charlton won 7-6 on penalties) 1998

The lottery-style nature of the play-off system was never better displayed than by the outcome of this match. Having narrowly missed automatic promotion to the Premiership, Sunderland now had to beat Charlton Athletic, who had finished far below them in the table. In the sunshine at Wembley, the Rokermen chose a bad time to have one of their rare off-days.

Nevertheless, they still would have beaten Charlton comfortably had Clive Mendonca not been on superlative form and their

> *"Last time we got a penalty away from home,*
> *Christ was still a carpenter."*
>
> Lennie Lawrence,
> then manager of Charlton Athletic

defence gifted Richard Rufus a last gasp-equaliser to send the match to penalties. At 7-6 to Charlton, with both sides yet to miss a spot-kick and with sudden-death now in operation, it fell upon Sunderland's Michael Gray to enter his name on the scroll of infamy. His weak penalty was pushed away by Sasa Ilic, thereby sending Charlton into the Premiership.

Needless to say, they were immediately relegated the following season – and passed Sunderland on the way down.

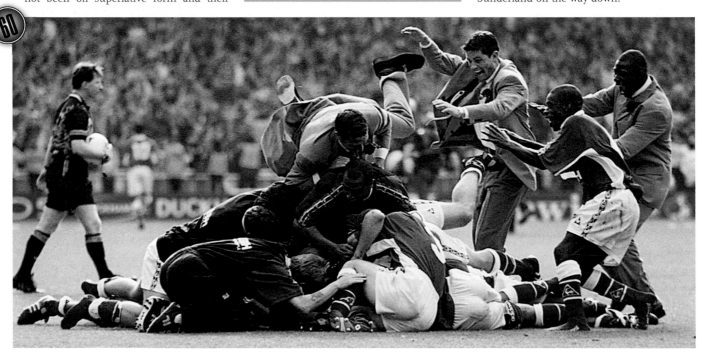

60

Left: Scenes of joy as Charlton's hero, goalkeeper Sasa Ilic, is buried underneath his team-mates.

Above: The other side of the coin, but Niall Quinn still loves Michael Gray

Hot Rod Eddie

Everton 3
Sheffield Wednesday 2
1966

Not until rugby league's Martin Offiah some 20 years later has such a clean pair of heels graced the Wembley turf. They belonged to one Eddie Cavanagh, a fanatical Everton fan, who was so ecstatic at seeing Mike Trebilcock's dramatic equaliser in the 1966 FA Cup Final that he set off on a one-man lap of honour across the pitch.

As the police cordon closed, Eddie showed breath taking evasive skills to dodge the long arm of the law. With the crowd roaring their approval, his *pièce de résistance* came as one officer grabbed hold of his coat – and Eddie simply took it off, leaving the copper clutching at thin air.

Eventually, after several side-splitting moments, Eddie was apprehended by no fewer than six policemen and ejected from the ground. Needless to say, he managed to sneak back in time to see Everton lift the Cup after Derek Temple's winner.

62

Yet more England penalty heartbreak

England 1 West Germany 1 (West Germany won 4-3 on penalties) 1990

After Paul Gascoigne's tears at being booked earlier in this match, thereby depriving himself of a possible place in the World Cup Final, and the utter joy of Gary Lineker's equaliser, it was Kleenex all round once again as England were knocked out of the competition in the penalty shoot-out. At first, it looked so promising: Lineker, Peter Beardsley and David Platt all scored. But so did Andreas Brehme, Lothar Matthaus and Karl-Heinz Riedle for the Germans. Up stepped Stuart 'Psycho' Pearce. Surely his trusty left boot would not fail the Three Lions. Disaster: the ball cannoned off keeper Bodo Illgner's leg.

Olaf Thon made it 4-3 to the Germans, leaving Chris Waddle with the do-or-die spot kick. The ball finished in the stand, and England were out.

Yet again the Germans beat England in a penalty shoot-out. Goalkeeper Bodo Illgner and Andreas Brehme celebrate as they go through to the World Cup Final

Stuart Pearce stands totally dejected after his penalty shoot-out attempt was saved by Illgner

Dogfight at the OK Corral

Burnley 2
Leyton Orient 1
1987

Burnley won this game 2-1, sparking a huge party among the 16,000 spectators crammed into Turf Moor. Yet the match was hardly a classic and before the game Burnley had been bottom of Division Four. The reason for the jubilation was that this was the first season of automatic relegation to the Conference, and it was a straight dogfight at the bottom between Burnley, Lincoln and Torquay for the drop. In the event, Lincoln went down – although it should have been Torquay.

They were trailing 2-1 at Crewe when a police dog ran on to the pitch and bit Torquay's scorer Jim McNichol. In the time added on for the stoppage, Paul Dobson scored an unlikely equaliser to keep the green and whites in the league.

Vinnie's on the ball

Wimbledon 2 Newcastle United 1 1988

Plough Lane, the scene of possibly the most famous piece of ball-work of all time as Wimbledon hard man Vinnie Jones got to grips with the precocious Paul Gascoigne in no uncertain terms.

The famous photograph turned both men into national celebrities.

"Well, stone me. We've had cocaine, bribery and Arsenal scoring two goals at home. But just when you thought there truly were no surprises left in football, Vinnie Jones turns out to be an international player."

Jimmy Greaves
on the shock call-up for the 'Welshman'

Squeeze until the pips squeak: Vinnie Jones shows Gazza where he got his reputation for being hard in the tackle

Cameroon KO

Cameroon 1 Argentina 0 1990

Although Cameroon would go on to prove they were no mugs, it was this World Cup Group B match against the champions Argentina that really put them on the map. For a start, they quickly made it clear that their tactics for dealing with the likes of Maradona, Batista, Caniggia and Burruchaga was to kick them off the park. After 61 minutes, when Kana-Biyik was dismissed for a cynical foul on Claudio Caniggia, most people assumed that the skilful Argentines would go on to despatch the ten-man Cameroons.

Far from it: six minutes later, Biyik's brother Omam climbed high in the penalty area and headed down towards goal. Keeper Pumpido inexplicably let the ball bounce in off his knee. Cameroon hung on for an astonishing win – made even more remarkable by the fact that they had another player sent off later in the match.

Cameroon goalscorer Omam-Biyik is mobbed by his team-mates

65

'Maggie Thatcher, can you hear me?'
Norway 2 England 1 1981

It was a dismal performance: a 2-1 defeat by Norway. In fact, England's first ever defeat by Norway – a fact that did not go unrecognised by Borge Lallelien, the host nation's premier radio commentator, who launched into a frenzied monologue of unbridled patriotism.

"We are the best in the world," he began. "We have beaten England! Lord Beaverbrook, Sir Winston Churchill, Sir Anthony Eden, Clement Attlee, Henry Cooper, Lady Diana – we have beaten them all! Maggie Thatcher, can you hear me? Your boys took a hell of a beating! Norway have beaten England at football!"

Lallelien sadly died 10 years ago. But, say what you like about his outburst, it's unlikely that John Motson could have mentioned quite as many famous Norwegians.

England v Norway *factfile*

England's record v Norway

Played	Won	Drawn	Lost	Goals For	Goals Against
10	5	3	2	26	7

Biggest victory: 6-0, Oslo, 14.5.37
Biggest defeat: 2-0, Oslo, 2.6.93

Thoresen fires in Norway's second goal to secure his country's first ever win over England and spark the best radio victory celebration of all time

Giggs' goal

Arsenal 1 Manchester United 2 1999

Ryan Giggs leaves Adams and Arsenal down and out

Even before its dramatic finale, the FA Cup semi-final replay between Manchester United and Arsenal was a match to remember: United one-nil up, Roy Keane sent off, Arsenal equalising and then Peter Schmeichel saving a penalty from Denis Bergkamp. The best was waiting until last, however. There seemed to be no danger when Patrick Vieira's misplaced pass found Ryan Giggs on halfway.

The Welshman set off for the Arsenal goal, leaving the Gunners' defence in tatters. Into the penalty area, it seemed that Giggs had gone too far to the left. Instead, he used his trusty left boot to thrash the ball into the roof of the net past a stunned David Seaman.

Giggs' subsequent celebration – shirt off and waved above his head – was almost as memorable as the goal.

Young's 'professional' foul

West Ham 1 Arsenal 0 1980

68

The FA Cup Final had already seen a remarkable rarity: a goal scored by Trevor Brooking from a diving header. The Hammers were heading for victory, and deep into the second half it looked like they were about to not only make certain of the Cup but add to its rich history of romance when 17-year-old Paul Allen broke clear with only the goalkeeper to beat.

> *"Trevor Brooking floats like a butterfly, and stings like one too."*
> Brian Clough

He was denied by one of the most cynical of professional fouls when Willie Young, floundering for pace, stuck out a leg and brought the youngster crashing to the ground from behind. Amazingly, Young escaped with only a booking.

Paul Allen, victim of Willie Young's unpunished professional foul, won in the end and got his hands on the Cup

Best of all

Manchester United 4 Benfica 1 (aet) 1968

Extra time in the European Cup Final at Wembley, the scores locked at 1-1. Suddenly, George Best runs clear on to a long through-ball. As the Portuguese defence close in, Best cheekily nutmegs one of them before rounding the goalkeeper and rolling the ball into the net.

"It was like Roy of the Rovers," said Best, who added that the nut-meg fulfilled one of his ambitions. His other was to stop the ball on the goal-line and head it in. "But the keeper was a bit too sharp, so I thought I'd better not risk it."

Goals by Brian Kidd and Bobby Charlton sealed United's triumph.

George Best walks away with the European Cup after scoring a fantastic individual goal in extra time

69

Last-gasp Sunderland

Arsenal 3 Manchester United 2 1979

At 2-0 up with only four minutes left to play, Arsenal looked to be cruising to victory in the FA Cup Final. The stage was merely set, however, for one of the most dramatic climaxes in history.

Gordon McQueen pulled one back, then, amazingly, Manchester United equalised through Sammy McIlroy.

Straight from the kick-off, with just seconds remaining, Arsenal launched one last attack down the left-hand side through Liam Brady. Socks round his ankles, the Irish wizard dribbled deep into United territory and laid the ball left to Graham Rix. He launched what appeared to be nothing more than a hopeful ball across the penalty area.

Suddenly, as if from nowhere, Arsenal's afro-headed Alan Sunderland appeared at the back post and diverted the ball into the net with his outstretched foot.

He barely had the energy to celebrate the dramatic winner before the final whistle blew.

Alan Sunderland scores Arsenal's decisive third goal, immediately after Sammy McIlroy had equalised for United

The Scorpion
England 0 Colombia 0 1995

With his drooping moustache and King Charles hairstyle, Colombian goalkeeper Rene Higuita arrived for this friendly at Wembley determined to make his mark. Sure enough, when England's Jamie Redknapp sent an aimless ball into the penalty area, Higuita elected not to catch it but instead launch himself into a bizarre "scorpion" kick in which the ball was fired back over his head by his own heels.

> *"It was like Bruce Grobbelaar with hair"*
> Phil Thompson on Rene Higuita's 'scorpion' save

After the match, Higuita came over all cautious, advising anyone watching "not to try it at home".

England v Colombia *factfile*

England's record v Colombia

Played	Won	Drawn	Lost	Goals For	Goals Against
4	2	2	-	7	1

Biggest victory: 4-0, Bogota, 20.5.70
Biggest defeat: N/A

Colombian goalkeeper Rene Higuita's amazing 'scorpion' kick was one of the most extraordinary things ever seen at Wembley

71

Lionheart

England 0 Spain 0 (England won 4-2 on penalties) 1996

Missing that vital penalty in the semi-final of the 1990 World Cup against the Germans had cast an indelible shadow over Stuart Pearce. So it was a testament to his courage that he insisted on taking one of the spot kicks in the Euro 96 quarter-final shoot-out against Spain. Another miss would be disaster for England, catastrophe for Pearce. Psycho did not fail.

> *"I can see the carrot at the end of the tunnel."*
> Stuart Pearce, 1992

As his penalty smashed into the back of the net, Pearce turned to the crowd with an expression of almost maniacal relief and determination that summed up just what it meant to exorcise his demons.

England v Spain *factfile*

England's record v Spain

Played	Won	Drawn	Lost	Goals For	Goals Against
18	10	3	5	35	20

Biggest victory: 7-1, Highbury, 9.12.31
Biggest defeat: 3-0, Madrid, 15.5.60

Stuart 'Psycho' Pearce lived up to his nickname after succeeding in the penalty shoot-out with Spain in the Euro 96 quarter-finals

The Matthews Final

Blackpool 4 Bolton 3 1953

73

Stan Mortensen scored three goals and Bill Perry the dramatic winner for Blackpool – but it was their team-mate Stanley Matthews after whom this FA Cup Final was named.

Having been on the losing side in 1948 and 1951, Matthews was determined that his

> *"The last player to score a hat-trick in an FA Cup Final was Stan Mortensen. He even had a Final named after him – the Matthews Final."*
>
> Lawrie McMenemy

A jubilant Matthews reaches out to touch the Cup

third Cup Final would not be a third defeat. His brilliance on the day was summed up by his jinking run to the byeline and inch-perfect lay-back for Perry to score the fourth goal.

83

Phil Neal scores Liverpool's goal, but with the score at 1-1 after 120 minutes, it went to penalties

Bruce Wobble-aar

AS Roma 1 Liverpool 1 (Liverpool won 4-2 on penalties) 1984

74

Nerves were on a knife edge as the European Cup Final went into a penalty shoot-out. Liverpool were 2-1 down, and Roma's Bruno Conti had to score to settle the issue. Unfortunately for

> *"Just tell them I completely disagree with everything they say!"*
> Bill Shankly to a translator, when being surrounded by gesticulating Italian journalists

Conti and indeed fellow penalty takers Falcao and Graziani – they were up against the Reds' lunatic keeper Bruce Grobbelaar.

"Don't worry, boys – I'll put them off," Grobbelaar cheerfully remarked as he wandered down to the goalmouth. He was as good as his word. As Conti stepped up, he saw Grobbelaar crouching on his line, knees swaying and knuckles dragging along the ground. Conti blasted it over the bar.

Next, Falcao. The Brazilian began his run-up, but was fatally distracted by the

While Grobbelaar distracted the AS Roma players on their penalties, Liverpool could not be put off

sight of Grobbelaar gnawing the netting. Another miss.

Finally, Graziani, whose racked nerves were finally shattered by Grobbelaar wobbling his legs like a drunken sailor. Miss number three. Grobbelaar's team-mates, meanwhile, had not let the side down and by winning the shoot-out 4-2, won the European Cup once again.

Blundering Bonetti

West Germany 3 England 2 1970

Two goals up with 40 minutes to go, England pressed the self-destruct button on their World Cup hopes in truly unbelievable style in the quarter-final in Leon. So confident were watching English journalists of a win against Uwe Seeler's men that they were crowing "Auf Weidersehen" to German fans. They were right, of course – but not how they would have liked.

The turning point was a monumental blunder by keeper Peter Bonetti, who had come in as a last-minute replacement for the unwell Gordon Banks. In the 67th minute, Franz Beckenbauer beat Allan Mullery on the edge of the England penalty area and fired in a low shot. The ball seemed to surprise Bonetti for pace, because he appeared to dive over it as it went into the net.

From that disastrous moment, England were completely turned over.

A speculative back header from Uwe Seeler looped over Bonetti for the equaliser, and in extra time Gerd Muller completed the fait accompli by scoring the winner.

The upshot of the defeat was devastating. Moore, Hurst, Bobby Charlton, Bonetti, Labone and Newton would never play for England again.

Peter Bonetti must have wished Gordon Banks had been fit, after his error let West Germany back into a match England appeared to be winning with ease

Pele's cheeky chip

Brazil 4 Czechoslovakia 1 1970

Two defining moments of the World Cup in 1970 were provided by Pele. Ironically, on both occasions the master goalscorer failed to hit the net – but he gets nothing less than full marks for trying. The first, as we have seen, was his superb dummy against Uruguay. Earlier in the tournament, however, he almost brought the house down during Brazil's group match against the Czechs.

With the score at one-all, and with the half-time whistle about to sound, Pele had the ball in his own half.

He glanced up and noticed that keeper Viktor was off his line. The subsequent lob passed just inches wide of the post.

It was one of the great might-have-beens of football.

Moore's tackle
England 0 Brazil 1 1970

One of Pele's most prized possessions after a long and unrivalled career is the shirt belonging to England's Bobby Moore. "Two men who marked me were head and shoulders above any other defender: Beckenbauer of Germany and Moore of England – and the greatest of them was Moore," he remarked.

One tackle by Moore on Pele's team-mate Jairzinho in this World Cup Group 3 match is testament to why the great man thought so highly of England's skipper. Picking up the ball on halfway, Jairzinho raced into the England penalty area and was cocking the trigger when Moore slid in for a perfectly timed tackle.

Not only did he dispossess the Brazilian without giving away a penalty, Moore managed to stay on his feet and play the ball calmly out of defence to Terry Cooper.

Hero to hero: Pele and Bobby Moore exchange shirts after England's 1-0 defeat by Brazil in the 1970 World Cup Finals in Mexico

77

The Russian linesman

England 4 West Germany 2 1966

The 1966 World Cup Final, extra time being played. The stage is set for England's historic win. But first, an equally famous moment of controversy.

Ten minutes played in the first period of extra time; Ball beats Schnellinger to a long pass by Stiles and sweeps the ball across from the right-hand corner flag; Hurst beats Schulz to the ball, takes it down inside the box, and hammers it goalwards; the ball hits the bar and bounces down; Hunt wheels away with delight; the Germans claim the ball did not cross the line; the referee seeks the opinion of the linesman; the goal is given.

The linesman's name was Tofik Bakhramov, and from that moment on he will be for ever the most popular Russian in England. Unfortunately, subsequent analysis has revealed pretty conclusively that he was wrong – the ball did not fully cross the line.

England win the 1966 World Cup, partly due to a Russian's decision

78

88

Stan's solo special
Italy 0 England 1 1948

Only something special could possibly silence 85,000 passionate Italian fans in Turin, and England's Stan Mortensen did just that. From the off, the Italians were all over England like a rash. Keeper Frank Swift had already made two great saves to keep the visitors in the hunt.

Then Stanley Matthews picked up the ball on halfway. Slipping his marker, Matthews looked up to see his Blackpool team-mate Mortensen racing forward from midfield. The pass was perfect, and Mortensen galloped on. As the Italian defence closed him down Mortensen was forced further and further diagonally towards the right corner flag.

As England's attackers flooded the penalty area, Mortensen was almost at the by-line. Yet, running at full tilt, he began to fall. At the same time he managed to slice the ball with his right boot. From a near-impossible angle the ball curled over the head of Italian keeper Bacigalupo's head and into the net.

England v Italy *factfile*

England's record v Italy

Played	Won	Drawn	Lost	Goals For	Goals Against
20	7	6	7	27	23

Biggest victory: 4-0, Turin 16.5.48
Biggest defeats: 2-0, Turin 14.6.75, Rome 17.11.76

Super Stan: Mortensen benefited from Stanley Matthews' passes with Blackpool as well as England

79

Tardelli's face

Italy 3 West Germany 1 1982

'Conti, Scirea… and this is Marco Tardelli!' John Motson's terse description of the Italy's second goal against the Germans in the World Cup Final bears little resemblance to the expression of sheer joy on the face of the goalscorer. As one writer described it: "If you look closely enough, you can see the souls of 60 million Italians in Tardelli's face." Quite.

Italy won 3-1, after a gruelling run-in in which they had beaten the holders, Argentina; then the favourites, Brazil; and then the third-place winners, Poland. Their star was Paolo Rossi, who scored first in the Final, but the face of Italian football in 1982 was Tardelli.

80

Marco Tardelli's face tells the story as he celebrates victory in the 1982 World Cup Final

Schumacher's shocker

France 3 West Germany 3 (West Germany won 5-4 on penalties) 1982

Michel Platini watches as Patrick Battiston is carried off after the shocking challenge of Harald Schumacher

A match remembered less for the fact it was the first World Cup semi-final to be decided on penalties, but for a foul of quite horrendous proportions subsequently left unpunished by refereeing of the utmost cowardice.

Just over 55 minutes had gone and, with the score at 1-1, French attacker Patrick Battiston was clean through and bearing down on the West German goal. Out raced goalkeeper Harald Schumacher. Battiston beat him to the ball, but Schumacher brutally clubbed into him with a raised forearm.

81

The Frenchman was left with two smashed teeth and was so badly hurt that for a few moments there were fears that he might die. Eventually, he was stretchered off the field to receive oxygen.

Such was the sickening nature of the collision, it took several minutes to realise that the referee, Charles Corver of Holland, had not only decided to spare Schumacher a booking, he had not even bothered to give a free kick. Schumacher's felony was compounded after the match when he offered to pay for Battiston's teeth to be capped.

Gemmill's glory
Scotland 3 Holland 2 1978

By the time Scotland came up against their mighty Group 4 rivals Holland in Mendoza, their plans of World Cup glory were predictably as tattered as the tartan flags that drooped from the terraces.

The Scots had proudly arrived in South America as Ally's Army. But humiliation against Iran and Peru, plus the sending home in disgrace of Willie Johnston after a failed drugs test, looked like reducing them to a rabble. Amazingly, they could still qualify – but only as long as they could beat the Dutch in their last match by three clear goals.

Ally's Army had one last poke at glory, and in loyal footsoldier Archie Gemmill, they

Holland v Scotland *factfile*

Holland's record v Scotland

Played	Won	Drawn	Lost	Goals For	Goals Against
12	5	3	4	15	11

Biggest victory: 3-0, Glasgow, 11.5.66
Biggest defeat: 3-1, Amsterdam, 21.5.38

Left: Ally's Army are on their way – for a few minutes anyway. Having already scored a penalty, the determined Archie Gemmill wheels away to the delight of Kenny Dalglish and his team-mates, after scoring a fantastic goal against the excellent Dutch side and giving Scotland a qualification lifeline.
Right: Gemmill enjoys the moment and salutes the Scottish fans

had a man determined to give it a final try. The Scots poured forward, but despite hitting the bar and having a goal ruled out, they went one down through a Rensenbrink penalty.

On the stroke of half-time, however, Kenny Dalglish volleyed the equaliser. A minute after the break, Gemmill scored a penalty and then, on 68 minutes, the diminutive midfielder picked up a loose ball on the right of the Dutch area, came inside Jansen's lunge, beat Krol on the outside, and pushed the ball through Poortvliet's legs before curling the ball majestically over the advancing keeper. It was a sensational goal, and for three brief minutes it appeared that Ally's Army was on the march to a miraculous win.

Then Dutchman Jonny Rep hit a long-range thunderbolt which left Alan Rough stranded and Scotland were out of the Cup.

82

El Loco

Cameroon 2 Colombia 1 1990

83

The eccentric Colombian goalkeeper Rene Higuita was billed as El Loco – but his blunder against Cameroon in the World Cup went beyond pure eccentricity. It cost his country a place in the quarter-finals.

There was no score after 90 minutes of this second-round match – but then madness struck. Having already gifted a goal at the near post to Roger Milla in extra time, Higuita attempted to rectify the situation himself three minutes later by dribbling the ball up the touchline towards the Cameroon goal.

Milla simply dispossessed El Loco and ran on, with a broad grin on his face, to slide the ball into an empty net.

Higuita thought he was a good winger as well as a goalkeeper – and tried to prove it. Unfortunately, after being dispossessed by Roger Milla, who went on to score, Higuita's blunder was to deny Colombia progress into the quarter-finals of Italia 90

A costly goal

USA 2 Colombia 1 1994

84

There seemed no danger when, after 34 minutes, USA's John Harkes attempted an optimistic but inaccurate cross-shot. Luckily for him, Colombia's usually adept central defender Andres Escobar stuck out a leg and diverted the ball into his own net.

The USA went on to win 2-1 – the Colombians only scoring in the last minute. Colombia were a shadow of the force they had once been, and the USA deserved to win even without Escobar's intervention.

Little did Andres Escobar know that this own-goal incident was to cost him not just the match, but, shockingly, his life

Yet his was destined to become the most infamous own goal in footballing history when, 10 days later, he was shot dead in Medellin – apparently because his blunder had cost a Colombian drug baron a bet.

Emerald glory

Republic of Ireland 0 Romania 0 (Ireland won 5-4 on penalties) 1990

Having progressed, along with England and Holland, from the 1990 World Cup's dire and aptly-named Group of Sleep, the Republic found themselves in a nerve-shredding penalty shoot-out against the Romanians in order to progress to the third round. With the scores at 4-4, up stepped Timofte to try and beat Ireland's talismanic goalkeeper Packie Bonner from the spot. Bonner palmed it away to great jubilation – but now it was up to David O'Leary, a central defender with no penalty-taking pedigree, to win the match for the Irish.

Showing nerves of steel, the rangy O'Leary made absolutely no mistake, provoking scenes of unbridled joy amid the emerald-draped hordes in Genoa.

Above: Pat Bonner saves a vital penalty before David O'Leary seals victory for the Irish by converting the final penalty. Needless to say, a few pints of Genoa's best Guinness were sunk that night

Haan's howitzer

Holland 2 Italy 1 1978

Having already scored a stunning 35-yarder against the West Germans, Holland's Arie Haan did not keep his fans waiting long for an even better sequel. Against the Italians in Buenos Aires, the scores were level at 1-1, after Ernie Brandts had equalised his earlier own goal for the Dutch.

With 15 minutes remaining and the reward of a place in the World Cup Final looming, Haan picked up the ball in midfield and from fully 40 yards out unleashed an absolute pile-driver straight into the top corner.

A week earlier, it had been the esteemed Sepp Maier who had been left rooted to the spot. This time the statuesque keeper was the equally respected Dino Zoff.

86

Holland v Italy *factfile*

Holland's record v Italy

Played	Won	Drawn	Lost	Goals For	Goals Against
13	2	5	6	14	19

Biggest victory: 3-1, Rotterdam, 20.11.74
Biggest defeat: 3-0, Milan, 24.2.79

Koreans have the last laugh

North Korea 1 Italy 0 1966

Gianni Rivera shoots at goal in an attempt to equalise against North Korea in 1966 and salvage some honour for the Italians

Prior to their famous meeting at Middlesbrough's Ayresome Park in World Cup Group 4, one Italian scout likened the North Koreans to a side made up of 11 Charlie Chaplins.

The Italian public failed to see the funny side when their team became the fall guys in one of the competition's greatest upsets.

Three minutes before half-time, with the Italians down to 10 men, Park Doo-ik collected a misdirected defensive header. From the edge of the box, the diminutive striker fired in the shot which beat keeper Enrico Albertosi. The North Koreans managed to hang on to their lead throughout the second half to record a famous win.

The Bald Bullet

Bulgaria 2 Germany 1 1994

Goals don't come much sweeter than this. One goal up through a Matthaus penalty, it seemed only a formality that the dour Germans would progress to the semi-finals at the expense of Bulgaria. But on 75 minutes, the Bulgarians' inspirational Stoichkov fired in a free-kick to level the scores.

Three minutes later, the Bulgarians administered the killer blow when Yankov broke free on the right and sent over a superb cross which the bald-headed Letchkov reached with a spectacular dive to send the ball into the back of the net and the Germans crashing out of the tournament.

The Bulgarian Bullet scored a beauty against the Germans – and doesn't he know it?

88

Collymore seals a classic

Liverpool 4 Newcastle United 3 1996

The last throw of the dice: Collymore blasts a spectacular goal to clinch a spectacular match

Everyone watching this Premiership clash had spent most of the game on the edge of their seat as advantage swung from one side to the other. Fowler! 1-0. Ferdinand! 1-1. Ginola! 1-2. Fowler! 2-2. Asprilla! 2-3. Collymore! 3-3... It looked to be heading for an astonishing draw.

In the 90th minute, however, Fate still had one last card to play. Newcastle failed to pick up Stan Collymore on the left, and the shaven-headed Liverpool striker hammered the ball left-footed past a helpless Pavel Srnicek for a dramatic victory.

"It's there to remind our lads who they're playing for, and remind the opposition who they are playing against."
Bill Shankly
about the 'This is Anfield' plaque

Nayim's lob

Real Zaragoza 2 Arsenal 1 1995

*I*t's the last minute of the Cup Winners' Cup Final in Paris. The score is 1-1. Nayim, former player with the Gunners' arch-rivals Spurs, has the ball on the halfway line. David Seaman is off his line. Nayim lobs him from 60 yards out. Seaman frantically backtracks. The ball drops fractionally under the bar and into the net. Seaman follows it in, his humiliation complete.

Above: Seaman needed consoling after being lobbed by Nayim from the halfway line and losing the Cup Winners' Cup Final in the last minute.

Right: The dreadful moment for Seaman when he realises that he cannot get back in time to stop the ball going into the Arsenal net

90

Narey's goal
Brazil 4 Scotland 1
1982

In this Group 6 match in Seville, the Brazilians were simply awesome. Scotland were destroyed, but any side would have failed to live with Falcao, Socrates, Eder and Zico that day.

Yet arguably the goal of the match was scored by Scotland's defender David Narey after 18 minutes. From Souness's crossfield pass, Wark headed the ball into the path of the charging Narey who, after a less than perfect first touch, hit an absolute screamer from 25 yards into the top right corner.

It was only Narey's second international goal, and for a few minutes it inspired thoughts of a famous victory. Then Brazil scored four.

91

David Narey strikes an unstoppable 25-yard shot to give Scotland an unlikely lead

Six-minute madness

Argentina 1
France 0

1930

With six minutes to go in this match during the first World Cup tournament in Uruguay, Argentina led by a goal to nil.

Suddenly, France's Marcel Langiller raced the length of the field and seemed certain to equalise. To his astonishment, before he could fire off a shot, Brazilian referee Almeida Rego blew the full-time whistle.

Mayhem ensued, as Argentinian fans invaded the pitch and the French team argued that there were six minutes left. As mounted police endeavoured to clear the pitch, Senor Rego consulted his linesmen and finally threw up his hands and admitted his error.

Meanwhile Cierro, the Argentine midfielder, fainted, the game resumed and the remaining six minutes passed without further incident or goals.

Over the bar

Italy 0 Brazil 0 (Brazil won 3-2 on penalties) 1994

They called him The Divine Ponytail on account of his dinky hair attachment. But in the penalty shoot-out to decide the winner of the 1994 World Cup, Roberto Baggio was a donkey. With the score at 3-2 in penalties to the Brazilians, Baggio needed to slot home the spot-kick to keep his side in the match. Instead, he hoofed it high over the bar.

93

Despair for Roberto Baggio after he had previously done so well for Italy in the 1994 World Cup Finals

Rivelino's free-kick

Brazil 1 East Germany 0 1974

Four years after lifting the World Cup in Mexico, the Brazilians were a pale shadow of that great team. However, in Rivelino, they had one of the great free-kick specialists.

His goal against the East Germans was typical of his style: a right-foot thunderbolt from 30 yards, aimed specifically at Jairzinho in the wall – who ducked as the ball flew over his head and straight into the corner of the net.

Rivelino was on the winning side in the 1970 World Cup Final, in which Brazil beat Italy 4-1. Four years later, despite his wonder goal to beat East Germany, his team failed to make the Final

94

Stepney saves

Manchester United 4 Benfica 1 (aet) 1968

With normal time ticking away, the 1968 European Cup Final was heading for extra time at 1-1. Suddenly, the unthinkable happened. Some slack midfield play allowed Benfica's dangerman Eusebio to race clear towards the United goal.

Stalwarts like Bobby Charlton and Pat Crerand could hardly bear to look as the striker pulled the trigger. Yet, somehow, goalkeeper Alex Stepney managed to fling himself at the ball and hold on to the shot. Even Eusebio was staggered by the save, and magnanimously took the opportunity of congratulating the United keeper immediately afterwards.

And it was Stepney's long kick that set up George Best's immortal goal two minutes into extra time as United won 4-1.

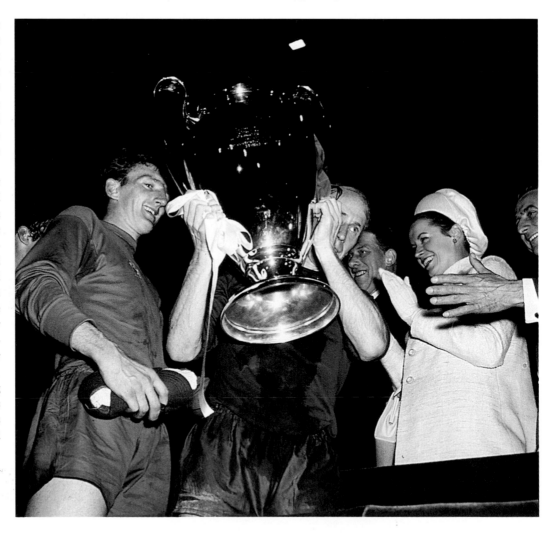

Alex Stepney stands alongside United captain Bobby Charlton as he lifts the European Cup

A Charlton thunderbolt

England 2 Portugal 0 1966

*I*f the 1966 World Cup Final belonged to Geoff Hurst, then the semi against Portugal was Bobby Charlton's. After 30 minutes, Charlton stroked home the opening goal after some good work by Roger Hunt. Simple stuff – and with Portugal's genius, Eusebio, being stifled by Charlton's Manchester United colleague Nobby Stiles, England held sway.

Then, on 79 minutes, Bobby Charlton the Wembley crowd to one of the all-time great goals. Hurst was the provider, racing on to Cohen's long through-ball and playing it back to Charlton, who was lurking outside the penalty area.

With barely a second thought, Charlton lashed the ball with phenomenal power into the roof of the net. Pereira, the Portuguese goalkeeper, never even saw it.

96

England v Portugal *factfile*

England's record v Portugal

Played	Won	Drawn	Lost	Goals For	Goals Against
17	9	6	2	39	18

Biggest victory: 10-0, Lisbon, 25.5.47
Biggest defeat: 3-1, Oporto, 22.5.55

Whether Bobby Charlton played on the left wing, as an inside forward or as a centre forward, his skills were unmatched and his cannonball shot was lethal

A proper Charlie

Arsenal 2 Liverpool 1 (aet) 1971

97

Extra time in the Cup Final. The ball is played to Charlie George, Arsenal's flamboyant, long-haired frontman. Socks round his ankles, George summons up one final burst of energy to send a shot into the corner of the net from outside the penalty area. Lying on his back, too exhausted to get up, George lifts his head and spreads his arms in triumph. The lad has just devised the most famous celebration in FA Cup history.

The most glorious moment in Arsenal's history: Charlie George, the hero of the North Bank fans, scores the goal that clinched the League and FA Cup Double for the North Londoners with just nine minutes of extra time remaining

Hagi magic

Romania 3 Colombia 1 1994

More than 90,000 people were crammed into the Pasadena Rose Bowl for this Group A match during the 1994 World Cup. They witnessed a comfortable Romanian win and a cracker of a goal by their playmaker and captain Gheorghe Hagi.

Receiving the ball on the left-hand touchline, Hagi looked up and, seeing the goalkeeper slightly off his line, hammered it with his left foot straight into the right-hand corner of the goal.

98

A happy looking Gheorghe Hagi, scorer of a sensational goal that lit up the 1994 World Cup

Ramsey's fury
England 1 Argentina 0
1966

The Argentinians came to England in 1966 with what appeared to be the sole game plan of kicking all opposition off the park. It led to a famously brutal encounter at Wembley in the quarter-finals which culminated in the Argentine skipper Antonio Rattin being sent off after half an hour. Rattin refused to walk. Then his team-mate Albrecht signalled that if the captain went, then the rest of the side should follow. After eight minutes of mayhem, Rattin finally left the pitch – but even then he had to be persuaded not to sit on the touchline by the police.

England won the game, but it left a sour taste in the mouth. Afterwards, manager Alf Ramsey – having prevented George Cohen from exchanging his shirt with Gonzalez – compared the Argentinian side to animals.

99

Off he goes: Rattin gets his marching orders

Cubillas kills off the Scots

Scotland 1 Peru 3

1978

When Joe Jordan gave Scotland a 19th-minute lead in the first game of the 1978 World Cup campaign, it seemed that all the hype about Ally's Army winning the trophy might be more than hot air. Yet from that moment on, the Scots utterly disintegrated. Cueto levelled the scores just before half-time, and then 29-year-old Teofilo Cubillas decided to run the show.

In the 70th minute, Peru were awarded a free kick some 30 yards out. Unfathomably, the Scots decided to stick Lou Macari – their shortest player – on the end of the wall.

Cubillas gratefully aimed his rasping, outside-of-the-boot shot over Macari's head and into the back of the net.

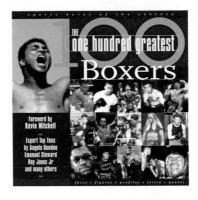

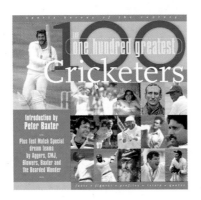

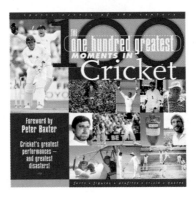

Available now from Generation Publications

(020 7403 0364)